T0353702

Legacy Song

Albert J. Corey

authorHOUSE

AuthorHouse™
1663 Liberty Drive
Bloomington, IN 47403
www.authorhouse.com
Phone: 833-262-8899

Published by AuthorHouse 10/25/2024

ISBN: 979-8-8230-3409-8 (sc)
ISBN: 979-8-8230-3408-1 (e)

Library of Congress Control Number: 2024920932

Print information available on the last page.

Any people depicted in stock imagery provided by Getty Images are models, and such images are being used for illustrative purposes only.
Certain stock imagery © Getty Images.

This book is printed on acid-free paper.

Contents

Other books by Albert Corey

This book is dedicated to our Lord Jesus Christ without whom I wouldn't be here, and I would not have been given any purpose or road to follow in this life. He gets all the honor and the glory.

I want to say THANK YOU to Beth Ferris, a special friend who helped me put this book together and who has a knack for finding the things I for some reason constantly miss.

Also, a shout-out and love to Pastor Chip McGee, Worship Leader Lindsey McGee and Celebrate Recovery Pastor Brian King without whose dedication to the ministries at our church I would not have been inspired to write some of the poems included.

To Create

Standing against a world of darkness
With no words at my command
Just a desire to create something
To add more beauty if I can
Not because it will be better
Than anything written before
More like a new instrument
Never heard at all
Wanting to join the band
Not to be the star
Just wanting to add another note
To the melody or harmony bar
Hoping others will understand
Wanting to say, "I was here"
Before this precious life I have
Disappears

The Song

Do not let the song go out of your life.
Fight with all the strength you have.
For once the song inside you dies
And the words no longer rhyme,
Your song will lie on the Cutter's floor,
And there will be . . .
No more time

You Never Know

Cherish all your friends
Admire the works of God
Dance while you can
Befriend a stranger
Lift up the poor
Love the unlovable
Pray without ceasing
For you never know
What life will bring
And rarely
Get to know why

When We Die

When we die
In those years by and by
What is left to mark our time
Our sojourn in this place?
Will there be signs
To say we passed here
Or did anything change
At all?

Forward

As age sets in some things tend to concern us more than when we were young. We are not able to do some of the physical things or remember many of the things we could easily do before. As we get older our reliance on God feels like it needs to increase, but it really should still be the same if we have been following Christ and relying on Him all through our lives. We should continue to praise God and thank Him for all the things in our lives: our health, our welfare, the air we breathe, the lives we have lived and the life still ahead of us. The biggest thing age should remind us of is that now we have less time to serve God than we did yesterday. (Hebrews 4:9-11)

I'm at the time of life where my thoughts and ideas, though looking like those of my past, have taken on a new urgency and life. The things I thought were important to me, and some still are, have decreased in importance or disappeared altogether. My friends, both past and present, have woven their way in and out of my life leaving cherished memories, both good and bad, which helped shape me into who I am today.

One thing I did learn along the way was there are always going to be people in our lives, some briefly, some for most of our lives be they friends or sworn enemies, acquaintances, people we do not even know, etc. who are going to see what you have, how you are considered and whatever power and/or fame you may have who are going to criticize and belittle you behind your back no matter how you may be treating them. We can choose to let it wear us into the ground or we can go to the One who always loves us and cares about what happens to us and give it all to Him. We, for our part, must constantly forgive and move forward knowing that God has this! Always remember, there are also people who say good things about you behind your back and/or praise the work that you have done. Many times, you just don't get to hear it. (Bummer!)

At my current age I find myself looking at circumstances in new ways.

Where once I would go crazy if something happened that I didn't like, I find that now it's not bothering me that much at all. Not that some things aren't worthy of consideration, they are, but I'm not going to waste the time worrying about them more than they need. I want to spend time on what really counts. My priorities are shifting, and that's been a good thing.

I read all the time on how 50 is the new 30 and 70 is now the new 50. People in their 50's and 60's, (probably the ones who started those ideas in the first place) are starting new careers and going off on fun adventures. My parents and their parents would never think of doing anything like that as they got older. Their idea of an adventure was to get together with other relatives to celebrate their children's birthdays or drive fifty miles (pretty much maximum) or so to see distant relatives and then come straight back home. Many of them never left the state they were born in. What they hoped would be there when they retired was children who would love and support them in their old age.

Our generation, on the other hand, loves to move around (we can't sit still), see the world and experience new things with no thought (other than whether we can afford it or not) of the time or the age we currently are. Granted, we have the luxury of faster, more convenient travel options, and depending on the price of travel (which can vary/escalate a lot!), can go to a great many places.

Some of the advantages our parents and great grandparents had was that the family usually didn't move that far away so they were able to stay in physical contact and were able to play into each other's lives (sometimes for the better, other times, not so much). Now, we stay in contact using various on-line methods over vast distances as if they were right there. The physical connection is pretty much a thing of the past (which is a sad thing when you need someone to be there with you while you go through something or to celebrate with you when something goes well). It's the little moments that happen unexpectedly that we miss out on. Sure, we take videos of some of them, and that's great, but it's not the same as being there.

As I was deciding the theme for this book, I began to realize that maybe I should write about a time in my life I had never written about before and that is - getting older. I've been experiencing this time of life for a while and other than the medical challenges that come along with aging, I love it. There are plusses and minuses to aging that I must learn as I wake up each day and I'll cover some of them as the book progresses. I have also come to realize that a lot of what I've written currently, poem wise, deals a great deal with my present age.

So, here we go. Hope some or a lot of it relates to what you may be going through now. Always remember you're never alone.

As with my previous books, I've included haikus at the beginning of each chapter. For some reason, I love writing these. Trying to get a thought or an idea across using the 5-7-5 syllable lines is always a challenge.

Chapter One

Learning

The life that you live
From one point to the other
Leaves a trail of you

Nights will only last
As long as days stay away
So, pray for the dawn

Sail your ship through life
Let God set the wind to lead
Sleep secure at night

Hope's the beginning
Reality is the end
Love is the journey

Some of the things you think about once you retire are centered around what you have done with your life, where you have been and all the people that you've met along the way. Then you think about the places not seen, what you may have done better, or how many lives you have influenced or have been influenced by over the years. The mistakes along the way come up too . . . some of course were our fault while others were done to us . . . don't dwell there, it's not worth it.

Most of all, and this is important, if you feel that you've done enough and it's time for the younger generation to take over because you feel you can't keep up . . . throw that idea into the deepest part of the nearest ocean you can find. It's hard enough that they think you are old and therefore useless (or at least, not as helpful), but it's worse if you think so. (Even more frustrating if your children or other family members think so)

Life must always be lived right up until God says I need you up here with me. When I leave here someday, there will always be projects that I'm still working on, places that I still want to get to, and people that I still want to meet. I wouldn't have it any other way! Besides, someone else will get to finish my projects for me! (if they find the time or want to, that is) :>)

Every minute we live is precious . . . a special gift from God, for which, I thank Him every day! We can never, ever, take it for granted!

When a Child is Born

When a child is born
A light appears
A lonely candle
Clinging to life
Fragile at birth
With numbered years

When a child is born
Its life is set
God creates us all
His light can shine in us
If we allow it
Nothing more, nothing less

Lantern

Lantern, lantern on the wall
Light the darkness away
Chase the things that rule the night
Keep them all at bay
Issue forth your radiant light
Save me from the things
That kill, steal and destroy
While I sleep the sleep of kings

Just Once Before I Die

If I could have a piece of the sky
Just enough for me to fly.
To rise above
The clouds I love,
If once before I die.

If I could sail a ship of yore
Just enough to reach the shore
To sail across
And not get lost,
I would live forevermore.

If I could climb the mountain high
Just enough to touch the sky
Then I would know
My place in snow
Just that once before I die.

If I could see beyond the dare
Just enough to know what's there,
I'd forget my need,
And let God lead.
Then I would get somewhere

If only once while I have breath
To reach beyond my hopes
To make my dreams reality
To break these mortal ropes
And live a life of quality.

When

When we get old
We learn the secrets
We wished we knew
When we were young

Or Three

Everyone loves a rainbow
Everyone needs a star
Everyone has a dream
Or two
Or three

Chapter 1A

Decisions

Ever wonder if at various times in your life you would have made different decisions than the ones you made? Would you be where you are today? With the many roads that appear before us it is tough sometimes choosing the right one. The ones with all the glitter look great but may not be the way to go. Others look like paths I would never choose just because of the way they look but are the ones I should have taken.

In my life I would love to say I took the right road every time, made the right decision at every juncture, and took everything into consideration all the time. Well, that just didn't happen. Maybe it was lack of wisdom on my part (undoubtedly), not enough good input from friends (maybe), my not listening to the right advice when it was given (most definitely), following the wrong wisdom given by people for whatever reason (a lot because it sounded good at the time), impulsive thinking, or just being stupid (can't dwell there either). I could go on with the reasons things happened or why I did what I did, but the real problem was me. My focus was on the wrong place with not enough information to get there and not enough resolve to find the right way to go about things.

Ever want to go back and correct the bad decisions you made, get out a big shovel and clean up all the messes? In my case there are so many of them that I would need another lifetime (or a bulldozer) just to get it all done. Sometimes I wish they had had classes in school to teach us decision making . . . but I probably wouldn't have learned anything anyway with the attention span I had back then. Isn't it sad we only get one shot at this?

Isn't it strange that we don't learn to pay attention to good advice until we get older, and even then, many of us still don't. It's a short life to learn all we need to learn and then learn to apply it carefully to our lives.

A Little More Hurt

Than my eyes seem to show
A storm builds inside me
That no one seems to know
Things all around me
Rob my peace within
When my bomb does go off
The world that we know
May never be the same again

When You're Stung

When you're stung by
The thorn of a rose
You'll find beauty is
Not always loving
Not always kind
Not always what
You thought it would be

Every Once in A While

I have a photograph
A frozen place in time
No movement, no feeling
Just images familiar
Resting in my mind

I have a photograph
Of those no longer here
No movement, no feeling
Just an aching loss
Here in my heart

I have a photograph where
In fifty or a hundred years
No one will know
No one will care
No one will keep it
It will be tossed aside
To be lost in the ground

I know I should record
Things the picture shows
So, when I leave the Earth
Memories will carry on
But I probably won't

I have a photograph
That I keep in a book
Means a lot to me
To have it around
Just so I can look at it
Every once in awhile

I Close My Eyes

I close my eyes
It is you I see
Shining in the darkness
Where I used to be
Son light and brightness
In my world of sin
Exposing the mess
My life is in

Your Love is Enough

(Written with Lindsey McGee)

I am here on my knees
My hands lifted up
I know you can hear me
Your love is enough
The veil's been torn
Opened for me
No longer in bondage
Now I am free

It's Jesus in glory
At the right hand of God
I'm free from the shackles
The pain, and the rod
The cross is the answer
For all men to see
Freedom eternal
Now I am free

I see Love
I see Peace
I see Beauty
I see Grace
I see Jesus

I'll shout to your glory
Your joy is my strength
You're righteous and holy
You're beauty and grace
You pursued and caught me
You never gave up
I'll love you forever
Your love is enough

Chapter Two
Growth

The moon and the stars
Shine balanced in the heavens
Beautify the night

The song that you write
The road you choose to travel
Should show all God's love

Building up your wealth
As vultures eye your display
Stays here to decay

Live close to the truth
To brighten your place in life
Lean closer to God

A good number of lessons I've learned (and am still learning) in life were learned the hard way (sad, but true). I read that one of the best ways to get a mule to do what you want him to do was to hit him between the eyes with a 2 x 4 piece of lumber. I was one of those. If I could go back and correct some relationships, I'd do it in a heartbeat! All those chances I had in life to say or do the right thing were messed up by my decision making, thinking "I Got This!" My focus was on the wrong place! Thinking things through was not one of my strong points (if it was one of my points at all). People who were collateral damage because of this were some of the ones who chose to leave my life, some for good. It was no one's fault but my own. It breaks my heart sometimes thinking about it.

Jericho

(from a sermon by Chip McGee)

How far will we have to walk
Before the walls begin to fall
Do we walk in boots or sandals
Or wearing no shoes at all
Are you making your own path
Or are you listening for the sound
Do you know the right direction
Or are you circling round and round

Have you prayed to find the road
Or have you used your time in fear
Clouds are watching, wondering when
The ancient roads for you will appear
Just like permanent marking stones
That show the borders of time
Seek and you are sure to find
A life filled with love Divine

A Beam of Light

Shine your light
Gently on me
A beam of light
For all to see
Lifting my soul

A Tree of Red

(inspired by a photograph by Chip McGee)

A tree of red
Appears in a sea of green,
Beneath a sky of blue
There is no sound
No other purpose
Than for you to see,
Changes that can be
When you allow God
To work in you

Byroads

A golden, narrow road
To get from here to there
The road built with loving hands
A road both straight and fair
And while it promises life,
Heavenly life, eternally,
We, instead, add byroads,
To travel where we please

Our byroads became gods,
Becoming our "pies" in the sky
Filling each of our minds
Leaving our hearts to die
No promises were ever made, yet,
We traveled on just the same,
And like the "gold" of rainbow lore
Our running was in vain.

Sad is the plight of human beings,
Who live their lives as they please,
Who can't see past the next "best thing,"
Whose only goal is "me."

Here

Wherever you stand is here
Travel two feet
Or two miles
If you try to return to here
You will find
It's not the same.
It will never be the same.
Here travels with you
A shadow in sunlight
A longing in your heart
To be there
When you get there
You are here.
Can you get there from here?
Or is here where you will stay?

Waiting For Change

It is like trying to stand
Between drops in the rain
Or climbing up a mountain
Standing on your hands

Like a stick in the river
Trying to flow up the stream
To the base of a waterfall
Drowning all your dreams

Like a penny on the track
Waiting for a train to come
Unable to move, unable to flee
Staring up at the sun . . .

Is waiting for change to come
Or worrying about the end
Standing in front of a door and
Never reaching out your hand

Seeds in the Wind

Seeds in the wind
Floating where they will
Falling to the ground
Gliding and dancing
Spinning around
Falling on roadways
Falling in fields
Falling in dark places
New harvests to yield

Unseen forces
Moves them around
Aloft in the air
Twisting and turning
Flying without care
Some land in briars
Some land on stones
Some are forgotten
Forever unknown

One chance to fly
No turning back
It's your race to run
Planning and scheming
For storms will come
To kill off your dreams
To kill off your visions
To kill off your hope
Beyond all reason

Soar while you can
Sing with the stars
Dance with the breeze
Rising and falling
Fly where you please
Seek out God's love
Seek out the way
Seek out the truth
While it is still today

Baptism

Water above you
Water around you
Lifting you
Sinking you
Loving you
Cleansing the soul
Inside and out

The world will know
The change in you
You were bought
You are saved
You are loved
Your soul is cleansed
Inside and out

Chapter 2 A

Second Chances?

That's the way I handled decisions in my life early on. I let the environment, the people or the events decide what I was to do next. Like the stick in the stream, I floated with the current and if I connected with something, and it turned out good, it would be totally by accident. If things went bad (a good deal of the time), it was a bad connection. I figured that was the way life was. I never gave it much thought.

Second chances are the things of dreams!

How Fragile

How fragile is life,
Trust and love.
How fragile is peace,
A gift from above.
How fragile is hope,
Grace and truth.
How fragile is faith,
The unseen, new

Does Anyone . . .

Does anyone know
Who opens the gates of time?
Does anyone care
If truth haunts driven minds
Does anyone want
A way to break the chains
Does anyone dare
Cut the ribbon of fame

Does anyone try
To hold the weight of space
Does anyone stand
When the enemy's in your face
Does anyone cry
When bells no longer chime
Does anyone trust
That it's all done in God's time

Does anyone hope
That tomorrow trumps today
Does anyone go
When it is safer just to stay
Does anyone love
Others, more than self
Does anyone pray
Not to be left on the shelf

Chapter Three
Changes

Fight foes if you must
Stand your ground to wage your wars
Win or lose, you hurt

Freedom comes with cost
Sacrifice and pain with care
Love requires effort

Come closer to truth
Run away from the darkness
Live your life in love

What are your values?
Do people see how you choose?
Can you change the world?

When my world exploded around me (did it ever), I had to face some hard truths. I found out that you can only float along that river for just so long and then things begin to cave in (whirlpools), or crash all around you (waterfalls), and that is exactly what happened to me.

In one year, I lost my grandmother, my mother and by the end of the year I was divorced from my wife of 10 years who left with our two sons. I started out the following year alone for the first time in my life. I became responsible for everything in my life without a plan to go by. I didn't like that a whole lot and for a while I even tried to ignore it. Then I realized that I had to learn to reorganize my life and take hold of the direction my life was heading (do people even plan their futures when things have gone haywire? I didn't).

Finding myself alone I had to learn to do the finances (didn't have to do them until then) and do everything around the house (laundry, cleaning, and cooking) along with working my regular job. Some of you are saying, "Poor guy, not having to do all that for this long in your life." You can stop laughing now. I began to learn responsibility. It took a while, but things began to get done on a consistent basis and I felt like I was getting on my feet. I couldn't shake the feeling of feeling empty, though.

I had accepted the Lord into my heart around the age of seven, then again at thirteen (having learned a little more about it). How to live a daily, Christian life was never brought home to me. The people I heard in church were focused on saving people (extremely important) but they didn't teach much more after that (such as living as a disciple, relying on God, living a Christian life, becoming a follower of Jesus.). So again, I was sort of floating (in a different stream this time) with the current with no goals or destinations in sight.

After my divorce I knew things in my life had to change. Here I was at 33 years old and still floundering. My focus, it seems, had always been on me or on whatever the next thing was. So, I sat down and talked to the Lord and told Him that I needed to change my life and get my feet on a firm path leading to Him. I rededicated my life to Him then and there, and never looked back.

One

One life
One voice
One hope
One faith

One God
One love
One truth
One way

Forgiveness

Every dawn signals a beginning
Every dawn brings new light
Every dawn kills the darkness
And with it, the fear of night

Every day breathes life anew
Every day brings hope of love
Every day a chance to find
Our road set by God above

Every night brings peace to hold
Every night sums up what was true
Every night we tally the cost
And pray forgiveness anew

Yet a Little Love . . .

One small word
Can bring light from darkness
One small hope
Can bring life from death
One small thought
Can change a person's mind
One small vision
Can move tens of thousands
One small faith
Can bring substance from nothing
One small change
Can alter your dreams
One small voice
Can move a mountain
One small life
Can change the world
One small hate
Can ruin everything
Yet a little love . . .

Peace

There's peace in my mind
There's peace in my soul
There's love overwhelming
That never grows old
There's peace in my Savior
That never will end
I am putting my future
In the hands of my Friend

Will You Listen?

There is a place inside
Where few have ever been
Where wisdom speaks the truth
To save the hearts of men
It screams from the crossroads
The byroads and malls
To some it is just a whisper
Others never hear it at all

There is a place inside
Buried in the human soul
Touched only by eternity
With walls of iron and stone
Where we choose to live our lives
And keep wisdom in a stall
Where darkness hides the truth
As we wander around our wall

There is a place inside
Where someone built a road
A road walked only by faith
That can bring us safely home
We feel safe and secure within
Yet the walls must tumble down
Wisdom's calling out your name
Will you listen to the sound?

If You Allow

If you take the time
To remember me
I will be with you
No matter what
If you make room for me
If you allow me inside
I can be seen
In your darkest hours

Alone is for those
Who wish to be
For those who choose
To wallow in the mire
"Knowing" they are
Beyond all hope
"Knowing" no one
Will ever come
Choosing instead
To run toward a fire

You were not made
To be left alone
You were not made
To be a "Woe is me"
People come into a life
People walk out of a life
You are a conqueror
Do you know that?
When people come
Love them while they're here

When they go
Love them and the memory
That they leave behind
They will never want you
To do anything but seek God

If you take the time
To remember me
I will be with you
No matter what
If you make room for me
If you allow me inside
I can be heard
In your darkest hours
Will you listen to the sound?

Chapter Four
A Firm Road

To begin to know
To seek for the things of God
Lives out His wisdom

The oceans can roar
Up from the depths of their world
To the feet of God

Love is the answer
God's sacred love is the key
Through Jesus it's shown

To find your way home
Requires a road and a map
And the Lord above

It was not an immediate change, but there was a steady difference in the way I began doing things. The feelings of people around me began to matter more. The places I frequented changed. The people I hung out with changed. I found a new marriage (with God's help and direction) with a beautiful Christian lady and got into a great church that was teaching the Word, and I was adding, day by day, the information I had always wanted but never knew I needed. I added more and more Christians into my life and really began to enjoy my time because I now had a purpose and a goal, a direction I could follow, I was happy! God had put me on the road I was supposed to be on.

I wanted to learn more about the life I had chosen to live. I had memorized biblical verses when I was young and knew where each of the books of the Bible were because I competed in "Sword Drills" as a kid where the leader would state a Bible book and verse, and the first to find it stood up and began reading it. I even won my first, personal Bible (KJV) doing that but didn't read it much (had trouble understanding a lot of it). Up until this point that was the extent of my Bible and Christian life training. Reading it was one thing, but understanding it was something else altogether.

About two years later the church we were part of elected to become a satellite campus for Christian Life School of Theology (Beacon College) with prices I could afford. They offered college courses toward degrees in Theology through class time, tests and correspondence. I signed up!

God's Hands

God's hands have lifted me
Carried me from birth to death
My boundaries were set
And carved in stone
Before ever we met

The time we have is
Precious
Fragile
Numbered
What we do
With it
Will count in the end

Though God's hands carried me
Throughout my precious life
I made decisions
I rose, I fell
Did things that weren't right

God of mercy, God of grace
Lift me from the mess I'm in
I now choose Jesus
Forgive me, mold me
Help me to begin again

The River Will Always March

The river will always march to the sea
Stones will always bend its way
Trees will always grow near its flow
Birds above will always play
Moss will grow upon the rocks
Fish will always swim beneath
No matter what the circumstance
The river will always march to the sea

Stairs

(Begun at CR May 3, 2022, from messages from Brian King)

As one foot follows the other
You climb the stairs of life
Worn down by those before you
Who searched for truth and light

The end we seek is down the road
Believing, it may soon appear
While we seek to find
The strength to climb another stair

Each of us has a path to climb
This is the life we're born to live
Struggling and climbing, ever up
Hoping for what this life can give

Climbing alone is scary
We can slip, fall off the stairs
With no hands to hold you safe
From freefalling through the air

Faith is courage, courage is strength
To reach your hand with care
Fear is real, faith is stronger
If we are willing to share

As one foot follows the other
We climb those stairs of life
His hand can help you reach your goal
Hold the hand that God provides

U & I

U walk the road alone
I travel with a friend
U ignore the love of God
I can't live without it
U do everything for "me"
I do everything for U
U take things for granted
I thank God everyday
U look to fill your time
I look to eternity
U say God's not there
I say he's the source of all
U say that life's not fair
I allow God to direct me
U say I waste my time
I won't live any other way
U fall and no one helps
I fall only to be lifted
U say God is a crutch
I will always lean on him
U choose paths of death
I choose the path of life
U will live forever
I will live forever
Where?

A Journey

A journey from here to there
May be only a few steps
The destination, however,
Can make all the difference

For you may feel "safe" here
Full of your memories
No adventure needed
No reason for you to leave

There is fear in a journey
With unknowns at every turn
Why move from where you are
What more do you need to learn?

A journey found the new world
The road less traveled trod
And a prayer prayed for another
Made all the difference to God

It's a Long Way

It can be a long way
From a prayer to here
Or as short as
Love, long lost, found

For nothing is more precious
Then flowers in the Spring
Or as sad as a rose
Lying on the ground

An old friend appearing
Brings back memories
Or someone sorely loved
With no words left to say

Stars in the heavens
Bringing beauty to the eyes
Or storms on the horizon
Which can take them all away

A soul need not be lost
When a door becomes open
Or left behind in the rush
To be thrown and tossed about

For all things can happen
As the circles slowly turn
For night, can become day
If we will only learn

The Place Where You Stand is Yours

Write your name upon the ground
And stand before the wind
Carve your name upon the clouds
At that moment
At that time
The place where you stand is yours

Write your name upon the sand
And wait for the tide to come
Burn your name upon the sun
At that moment
At that time
The place where you stand is yours

Your name is written in a book
There by blood from one Divine
Your name will never be erased
At that moment
At that time
The place where you stand is yours

Chapter Five
Reaching Retirement

Flowers over moss
Are dancing in the moonlight
All to God's glory

To dance in the sky
To fly over blue-green waves
Is to live your life

Working for the goal
Praying you will get to see
A new beginning

Look to the future
Leaving yesterday behind
Living out today

I found that learning what is said in the Bible, the experiences and the lives of the people who lived through the stories and allowing God to speak to me through the Bible made that book come alive. I was so glad I made that decision to give my life over to the Lord.

So, time has passed, and now I'm approaching the "Golden" years and find that I have a bit more learning of a different kind to do.

Should I go the rocking chair route, hang out on a porch somewhere watching the world go by, saying to myself "I have nothing more to give or for that matter, want to give?" Do I stare at the walls and wonder how my world got so small? Now that I'm retired, what do I do now? Do I start to worry now that my health is not the same as it was 20 years ago?" This list can go on and on.

God has blessed me with a lot of interests (not that I'm THAT good at any of them) and it tells me in the Book of Galatians that to whom much is given, much is expected. That pretty much helps me to rule out the entire previous paragraph.

Mornings are different however, I still pray before I get up, I still exercise after I get up, I still do a mile and a half walking most days, then go downstairs to study before I start my day. I don't worry about the clock anymore because of retirement. Before I get up, I am a lot more thankful for being able to get up, and because I'm looking at a new day. The looks of the guy in the mirror have changed considerably but he'll get over it . . . I hope!

It's funny, the guy inside of me hasn't seemed to age that much, but the outside could use a little help! When people see gray hair and the additional wrinkles, assumptions are immediately made (true or untrue) which begins to restrict what people my age are allowed or expected to do.

Yesterday

My yesterday's grow in number
With each passing day
My tomorrows are more wanted.
More precious on the way

Yesterday is guaranteed.
Tomorrow, it is not.
The here and now is sacred.
Bake the loaf, fill the pot.

Yesterday won't come again.
As days turn into years
Do not focus on yesterday
It'll only bring you tears.

There is a Feeling in Autumn

There is a feeling in Autumn
Nothing tangible, just felt
The look of mist over colored leaves,
Babbling brooks and old graveyards
Crooked stone walls going nowhere.
Ancient dirt roads with glistening stones
Distant blue mountains, warm rolling hills
Wild geese in the sky singing on their way.
Orange and yellow accented with red.
Hoar frost on leaves early in the morning
Smells of bacon cooking floats in the air
Farmers and scythes out reaping the fields
Filling their barns for the long Winter ahead
There is a feeling in Autumn
Nothing tangible, just felt.

When is a Road Not a Road?

When is a road not a road?
If you're heading
Where you should not go,
Where ends are dark and unknown

When is a road not a road?
If you seek eternity lost
Where the road is filled with woe,
Where ends are dark and unknown

Roads are built with gravel
Some are built with stone
Some are built with pine and oak
Where seeds were never sown
Every road begins
Every road ends
The time you spend upon a road
Will be precious time
Given only once
Given to you
Until you pass around the bend

When is a road not a road?
If you're heading
Where you should not go,
Where ends are dark and unknown

Would You Ever Know?

When a willow walks through the meadow
Sunshine filters through its limbs
Leaving a trail that fades from view
Would you ever know?

When an eagle soars around the clouds
Weaving high above the rain
Leaves a trail that fades from view
Would you ever know?

When a rose lives alone in the forest
With the breeze carrying its scent
Leaves a trail that fades from view
Would you ever know?

When a poem written full of hope
And considered by a few who care
Leaving a trail that fades from view
Would you ever know?

Sometimes Grass Grows in the Road

Sometimes grass grows in the road.
Trying to find
What once was there.
On a road much used
And wagon wheels
Bearing their loads
Seeking other roads
Wore the land down.
Completely unaware.

Sometimes grass grows in the road.
Trying to find
What once was there.
What once was green.
And so serene
Where trees grew tall
A bluebird's call.
Breaking the silence.
Somewhere in the air

Sometimes grass grows in the road.
Trying to find
What once was there.
Should we look again?
There around the bend
Do we need this road?
To carry our loads
Or allow grass to grow
To find a forest again

Clouds

Clouds on the horizon
Float over a misty day
The leaves of trees long since gone
Lying on the ground to decay
Leaving the branches bare
As Autumn fills the day

Chapter Six
That Thing Called Mourning

Sorry for your loss
For ragged holes in your life
Left behind by friends

If you lose someone
And your world comes crashing in
Reach your hands to God

A death is final
It can be a beginning
Finding your way home

Silver in linings
Will help chase those clouds away
Finding gold in love

In many quarters being older keeps you from possibly being allowed to do certain jobs, activities, or things because you don't look the part anymore. Once you get past a certain age (whatever that is) you are no longer "current" or have anything left to give. You are told that you couldn't possibly know how to deal with things occurring now and you are too old to train or to learn or to understand. You volunteer to do one job only to find they'd rather use you elsewhere for their purposes or not at all. You will never hear that verbalized out loud in person. Like I said, I have a lot to learn! It can be frustrating at times not knowing what is really meant by the looks or the comments, whether intentional or not . . . most times you just don't know. They don't seem to believe that we might be able to check with ourselves first and decide whether we can do the job to begin with. It's like any other war- you choose your battles and keep your sanity.

The saddest thing about getting older that I have found is losing people around you, either going away or passing away. Whether they were lifelong friends, family or people you've known for only a couple of years, it hurts when they go (it happens when you're younger but more so as you age). Your mind battles with the fairness of it, the sadness of it, leaving you frustrated, and many times mad! I'm sure there are other people more deserving of dying but not "my" friend. People left behind will blame the circumstances, each other, a disease, or sadly, God. Some people equate age with dying thinking if people die young, "that should never had happened", whereas people who are older it seems to be expected. No matter what the age, dying would not be our first choice!

I was asked to do a memorial service for my Aunt Dutch (Bessie) which broke my heart. I had known her all my life and she always treated me well. She, more than anyone, encouraged the art and creative side of me and made me feel like I could do it. She would take the pictures I drew and hang them on her living room wall. A picture you create being put on a wall by someone who likes it at whatever age you are is huge. I shudder at what my earlier pictures looked like now, but at the time it didn't bother her at all. She even made my very first leftover turkey sandwich! (love those things to this day!)

Losing her . . . HURT! Over the years, one of the things I found out was that she loved flowers! It didn't matter if they were wild or domestic, she loved them!

Lady Slippers

(For Aunt Dutch)

I lay here and think as life slowly ends
While a stream nearby is flowing
Just the way it flowed when I was born
There's wonder there and sadness

The trees around it are bigger now
Moss has spread over their roots
Lady slippers dance among the leaves
With sounds of birds floating

I can no longer walk that path
Strolling among the trees and scrubs
To listen for those sounds in the woods
With clouds floating over my head

All those greens in the Spring, reds in the Fall
As breezes play in the branches
I feel them now through the open window
There's wonder there and sadness

There is a better place I'm heading for
That much I know is true
I pray there is a stream flowing there
Complete with moss covered with dew
And lovely lady slippers

Your Best Friend

A best friend is for life
A part of you within another
Someone who knows those things
That drive and motivate you
Who keeps you on your toes
And holds your heart in their hands
Who will cry before you do
If they know you will be hurt
Who stands up to anyone
To protect one hair on your head
Who finds a way to be there
As things crash around your shoulders
Who will listen 'til all hours
As you share every care you have
Who will laugh with you
And cry with you

So, there is nothing worse
Then when your closest friend
Leaves our earth before you do

The hole left is large
The hole left is ragged
The hole left is lasting
The hole left hurts
That part of you inside another
Can never come back
Can never be found
Can never be healed
Can never start again

Remember your friend never
Wanted to leave here first because
Part of them is there in your heart,
That part was their gift to you

Length of life is never known
Only God has planned your steps
Walk each step God blesses you with
Next to the friend
You never want to lose

Why do Flowers Weep?

Why do flowers weep in the valley?
When the sun sets in the west
Where at the end of the day
Will wither slowly away

Why do the days grow shorter?
When the years cease to come
Where calendars all die
Withering slowly by

Why are flowers pretty one day?
When seen by only a few
Winds cause them to bend
Withering in the dew

Why have lives that are short
When will this all end
Where at the end of the day
We won't wither away

You'll Leave Here Alone

Lay down your silver
Lay down your gold
You won't need it
If truth be told
As your life subsides
It's harder to hold
And when you leave
You'll leave here alone

Nothing in your hands
Nothing in your coffin
You'll leave as you came
Just flesh and bones
As your life subsides
It's harder to hold
And when you leave
You'll leave here alone

An Old Apple Tree

A deer stands
Under an old apple tree
That's been growing
A very long time
Standing alone
Some branches blown away
Leaving ragged scars behind

Wild twisted bark
Gnarled with age
Wild birds and insects
Call it their home
Wearing hearts of love
With just one dove and
Initials only lovers had known

Roots still hold
To the cold, dark earth
Firm from the storms
The clouds brought along
Memories uncounted
Remembered by the wind
Sung in a soft, soulful song

So, when you notice
The old apple tree
Peaceful and serene
Overlooking the land
Think of summer days
Two people in its shade
Planning a future hand in hand

Chapter 6A

Moving

When I moved south to the Carolinas from New York almost 9 years ago, I befriended a guy at church who handled the sound equipment and did it well. My wife and I couldn't be on the Worship Team (lots of gray hair and fat calves that can't wear skinny jeans), but we get to lead worship once a month on Thursday nights for our Celebrate Recovery gatherings. We had had all kinds of experiences with sound people in the past (some were great, some rather challenging), so it was a great relief to have someone who knew what he was doing. We became good friends during that time with similar interests in the outdoors and philosophy on life. We spent a lot of time talking about all kinds of things.

You didn't know him for long before you found out He LOVED hot sauce . . . on anything and everything! When I heard he didn't have long to stay here on Earth with us, I wrote this for him a couple of days before he beat me to Heaven. I miss him a LOT!

Top of the Hill (for Dave)

Let the raging waters
Wash the tears away
To the top of the hill
Where wind songs play
The lilies will dry them
And hang them to dry
To float in the breeze
As snow geese fly by

Tears are a question
To the silence we feel
Not a destination
To the top of the hill
A release from the rage
Is all that they are
Lilies live for a day
Then follow a star

Hearts can be broken
As friends are torn away
We'd keep them if we could
To live another day
They're off to see Jesus
In His arms they will stay
To a home built in Heaven
Where we'll be someday

Where those of us
Who choose to follow Jesus
Will all be living someday

Chapter 6B

Keeping Friends

Learning to mourn is one of the toughest lessons that older people (and younger ones too) need to learn. If they are Christians, they know where their friends or family have gone, but good friendships are hard to find and tougher when you're older, so it hurts just the same. It takes a lot to find and keep good friends when you get older. If you have someone, or many someone's, in your life now that you consider good friends, cherish them and never, ever, take them for granted. Do whatever you can to hold on and be there for them as they will hopefully be there for you.

Learning to Mourn

Along the shore I see birds fly
Silhouettes against a fading sky
The sun setting in the west
Waves crash along the sand
Pulling it back out to sea
I'm frozen, staring at the why

If I could turn and fly, I would
To float o'er the cares of this earth
If I could ride the sea, I would,
My back to the things of this world

I'm not mad, maybe a little sad
Just a little lost, a little found
Not bewildered, shedding some tears
Someone is gone
I'm learning to mourn

Look inside your heart of flesh
Past all the mistakes you make
See the one who loves you so
Loves you more than words can say

Someone is gone
I'm learning to mourn

Clinging

(From a Prayer by Lindsey McGee)

We love people
We lose people
Especially ones we love.
Cling if you can
Cling if you will
Cling if you must
In the end, they all go home.

Learning life without someone
With their shadow always there
Is a mountain no one wants to climb
A life no one wants to share
A hole inside a human heart
That no needle can repair
Leaving a pain you cannot see
Like separating fog from the air

Living life without someone
With all the memories there
That seem to live again and again
While you want to scream unfair
A scar inside a human heart
To be seen by all who stare
That never ever wants to heal
Always bleeding, always bare

If we love our Lord
We won't lose our way
Even on days like these.
Cling to His love
Cling to His strength
Cling to His might
In the end, you will find peace.

Though You've Passed from This Earth

You left behind the loves
To which you've given birth
Friendships lasting forever
Though you've passed from this Earth

Time was what you gave
Not something you held dear
Favorite memories come to life
Though you've passed from this Earth

You birthed dreams and plans
New ways to peace and grace
A living testament that we could see
Though you've passed from this Earth

May those who still stand here
Prefer the life you lived
Love you gave so graciously
Though you've passed from this Earth

Maybe Tomorrow

Maybe tomorrow
When things may be better
When focus may appear
The dawn may be brighter
At that time of the year

Saying "I love you" is easy
When you know
You'll do it tomorrow
Today there is too much
Too many miles to go

The demands of the day
Haunt you when you rise
Follow you around
Putting off something "easy"
Seems the right thing to do

They know I love them
They know that I care
Telling them tomorrow
Will mean so much then
I'll just finish off today

Here at the end of the day
Labors still not finished
Time has beat me again
Tomorrow I'll start all over
And finish them if I can

There is always tomorrow
Or is that really true?
Will I ever be finished
With so many things to do
Tomorrow will be better

Saying "I love you" is easy
When you know
You'll do it tomorrow
Pray they'll still be there
When all your labors are through

Summer Morning

Walking past a cemetery
While on my way to church
A man was standing by himself
In a peculiar sort of way

How strange to see a man alone
Standing in a place like this
Talking to a gravestone
As if someone else was there

He was nodding at the grave
And occasionally smiled
With grass and trees looking on
He was passing the time of day

Where I was, I couldn't hear
The things he had to say
Just sounds drifting through the air
On a bright summers day

Sounds of birds filled the trees
Rays of sunshine through the leaves
A man at peace in a graveyard
Filled my heart to overflowing

She Never Said a Word

Walking the widow's walk
Like Ellen used to do
I never understood
The tears in her eyes
'til I met someone like you

Spent all my summers
At her house by the sea
Where every day
She'd climb the stairs
To catch the ocean breeze

She loved all my yarns
I wrote to pass the time
Whether rain or shine
She'd listen to my words
As I made my poems rhyme

Those years full of wonder
Aunt Ellen at my side
Walking along the beach
With shells everywhere
Watching the flow of the tide

Now today I am alone
Aunt Ellen has passed away
My husband buried at sea
My books selling well
Her house is now my place to stay

She left me her home
With memories full of love
The stairs she used, they're
Dusty now with time
Leading to her place above

And so, I climbed the stairs
To see things from her stand
Remembering our times
We'd spent together
Walking along the sand

I stood alone for hours
'til I finally turned to go
A worn picture of a man
Hung on the wooden wall
Lit with the suns setting glow

I pull the picture from the wall
To see the writing there in black
"With all my love and blessings
My one and only Ellen
Please don't worry, I will come back"

She never said a word

Chapter 6C
Alone

There is a different kind of mourning that I hope none of you ever must go through, and that is, birthing a child knowing that they will one day be killed, or birthing a child who chooses to go away leaving you alone.

So many people in our country now have children who live all over the country or the world who can't or won't find the time to go home to see you. You wouldn't think this should be included in a mourning chapter, but aging parents go through a loss in their lives which also HURTS. No one wants to be alone if something bad happens in their lives and they have no family to depend on. (Ecclesiastes 4: 9-12)

The Bible talks about Mary pondering many things in her heart during and after the Wise Men left. I can't imagine what she must have thought. I've always wondered how much of the future of Jesus she knew, and if she did, how did she handle knowing it. I choose to see her dealing with things on a day-by-day basis and leaving the rest to God. For me, I can't think of any other way she could have possibly handled it.

Sleep Softly My Son

(For Mary)

Sleep softly my son
For you know why you're here
And though it be
A mountain to climb . . .
Tonight
You are safe
Right here with me

Sleep softly my son
For as your road lies ahead
That it would be
I could protect you . . .
Tonight
You are safe
Right here with me

Sleep softly my son
For love wins out in the end
If there could be
Any other way . . .
Tonight
You are safe
Right here with me

Sleep softly my son
The world will wait one more day
For though it be
A few minutes more . . .
Tonight
You are safe
Right here with me

Someone else in the Bible had to come to a decision to part with her son and risk having him killed if the authorities found out he existed. She set him loose on a river and left him to God. Not sure if I could have done that.

Jochebed

Floating by the shoreline
Hidden among the reeds,
And cattails
Alone on the water
Following the flow
And currents

At the mercy of the ebb
And flow of the water
So fragile
An old fraying basket
Bouncing from rock to log
Spinning 'round

Holding a secret treasure
Held in a tattered wrap.
So precious
The dreams of one, released.
To be picked up by another
Hopefully

O the pain of heartbreak
Split apart from your love.
Forever
Not assured of survival
Just a thread of a chance
At new life

Some people don't mind living alone, and at times, even prefer it. Many, however, don't.

When You Go Away

Will children bring you flowers
While you are alive
Or wait until the final day
When you go away

Will they bring you stories
To pass your time now
Or share them with each other
When you go away

Will they call to lift your day
Sharing love a few minutes
Or receive calls from strangers
When you go away

They leave your house in love
Ready to start their lives
Thinking you'll be okay
As they busy their time away

As days turn into years
Never thinking at all
Of the love you had for them
Before you went away

Lives must be lived out
All urgent things done
Does anyone want to hear from you
Before they go away

Alone

Living alone
Is challenge enough
Surrounded by the dark
And unknown dangers

A lifetime of loving
And praying the best
For the ones around you
And all the rest

When you want to share
The special things
You talk to the walls
That surround your life

So, you live your time
And wait for those calls
Silence reigns supreme
As years march along

The saddest thing
When you reach the end
Is being alone
With nobody there

Old Letters

Found a pile of old letters
Tied together with faded twine
Worn at the corners
Sent by a friend
That I knew long ago
Someone left in a corner of my mind

Found a pile of old letters
Filled with love and thoughts
Filled with memories
My friend is gone
Lost to the halls of time
Letters in my hand are all I have

Found a pile of old letters
Treasures of a bygone place
Filled with sadness and joy
A friend I loved
For years of my life
Who took the time to write

When Someone Cries Alone

When someone cries alone
The sound is never heard
Sadness, fear and grief
All pouring out at once

When someone cries alone
A future is hard to see
A friend is hard to find
The past close behind

When someone cries alone
Rain won't drown it out
Darkness falls around them
Invisible to the outside world

When someone cries alone
The well never runs dry
Tears, tears, and more tears
Reaching to the sky

When someone cries alone
Relief can be found
Just a prayer away
The Lord reaches a hand
To lift a sad soul out
To send them on their way

Chapter Seven
Dealing With Things

I cannot forget
The way things were yesterday
Life before the war

Reaching out for help
When the memories return
A life filled with pain

Life is fortunate
If you never have to fight
Never have to kill

Losing one who's close
To obtain a foot of grass
Causes one to scream

Once someone has gone out of your life, you begin the process of putting one foot in front of the other. There is no one to blame, there is only today and how to get through it. People will check on you for a while, but sooner or later, you must find a way to deal with it on your own. My way of dealing with loss was going to the Lord for as much help as I could get. It can still be a long process.

Some people, me included, lose people in a war, terrorism or armed conflict which becomes a different thing altogether. These people are violently yanked out of your life . . . not a great place for you to be. You feel helpless, violated. These are the type of losses which bring out anger in us and in some cases, retaliation. Don't go there.

No One Sees Us

No more walls to jump over
Or to hide behind
No more whistling sounds
Of death overhead
No more fear to twist your gut
Or shaking in your knees

That's what was said when the war ended
We were free to go home
With the guns and helmets left behind
Our memories came along

During our days we smile
And do the best we can
The nights are another matter
We scream awake in our beds
We're still jumping over fences
And hiding behind a wall
Hitting the ground at every sound
Watching fellow soldiers fall

We talk to those who care
Listen to what they say
We try the things they recommend
To get us through the day
When the sun goes down at night
As we lay there in our beds
We close our eyes, sights and sounds
Repeat, all over again

Time may be the answer
But it needs to tell us soon
Meanwhile we wait for rain
Which hums a calming tune
We walk among the raindrops
Falling through the gloom
For as we cry within the storm
No one will see us if we do

Feather on the Ground

A feather on the ground
Lying next to a stone
No longer free to fly
A life that's all but gone

Letters chiseled on a stone
With someone there below
No longer free to fly
Life is all but gone

A breeze may soon come
The feather will be gone
No one will ever know
Or hear the silent song

Battlefields

The soldier stood tall
Every button aligned
With boots that sparkled
His sword at his side
His horse was black
The saddle just shined
He was ready to charge
He was ready to fight

There on the battlefield
With others on the ground
Grey smoke in the air
And barely a sound
His uniform in shreds
His boots colored red
A surprised look in his eyes
His horse lays dead

When you go into battle
Determined you may be
Bullets may call your name
Wanting to win the battle
You forget to heed the sound
Of your name being called
Until a sting fills your senses
As darkness covers your fall

When a bugle sounds
A sword in your hand
Your horse at full gallop
As you ride with your band
Ears listen for your name
With your life on a thread
Will you stop what you're doing
Or will you join the dead?

Come to the Shelter

Come to the shelter from the gathering storm
Your kingdom is gone, your mind overthrown
Your home, security, have all blown away
Broken hearts, in pieces, exposed to decay

Winds are upon us; lights have gone out
Words ever louder, lies and more doubt
Peace is hiding, dark clouds growing
Killing and mayhem, idolatry soaring

Nothing left to do, no shapes, no forms
Friendships, once cherished, have left you alone
All the ladders you've climbed, have fallen to dust
All the precious metals, have now turned to rust

If you're tired of it all and looking for a cure
There's only one place left, one place that's sure
You'll live high on a rock, hidden from harm
Come to the shelter from the gathering storm

There's a Flower in the Field

There's a flower in the field.
Growing there on its own
No ambitions, no hopes
No other place to call home
A memorial to the lost
Buried there below
They had a future
They had a past
They had no choice
War is like that

Please

Please
Don't walk behind me
I love you too much
To let you do that
A life is meant to
Spend together
Solving the problems
Facing our lives
With no one in front
No one behind
Side by side
Till death do us part

The Little Wooden Cross

A Short Story

We ran through the night trying to put on the darkness so as not to be seen. We kept landing on things on the floor of the forest which made way more noise than we wanted. We could hear the shots being fired but we didn't look back to see where they were coming from. We just kept hearing the "zip" sound through the leaves or an occasional thud of a bullet hitting a tree trunk.

I don't know how long we ran but finally we didn't hear any more gunshots. We found a large stand of trees with some old fallen trunks and decided to hide there. After an hour or so there was nothing but silence, so we felt safe enough to eventually fall asleep.

When I woke up the next morning Steve was groaning so I went over to check him out. From the front he looked okay but as I got closer, I realized he was bleeding from his back!

"Steve, you've been hit?" I asked. There was more fear in my voice than I wanted to let on.

"I think so," he replied. "I thought I had gotten bruised when I fell over some rock while we were running. This morning, when I woke up, it hurt bad."

I slowly rolled him over and a bleeding bullet hole showed up under his torn shirt. It looked like he lost a lot of blood.

"Looks like you scraped it pretty good when you fell" (I stretched the truth a bit).

"You were always one of the worst liars I've ever run into," he replied half smiling. "Just how bad does it look? This time try to put a little more accuracy into it."

"Well, it's definitely a ticket back home once they get you patched up," I answered.

"You're getting closer, it's not good, is it?"

"I'm afraid not," I replied. "I have some medical stuff to clean and cover it, but that's about it."

"It's not much use patching up a hole once all the blood is gone, is it" He was still half smiling. "If you would, can you set me up a bit? I've something to tell you".

"Sure," I said as I gathered up some leaves to make him a little more comfortable.

"I have been carrying this most of my life and now that my time is ending, I want to give it to you. My father gave it to me when I turned 10 back on the farm where I grew up. Now I want to give it to you."

"What is it?" I asked.

"Help me get this chain from around my neck and I'll show you."

When we got it off, I saw a small, wooden cross attached to the chain. It looked pretty beat up with small gouges and nicks all over it. I couldn't understand why he wouldn't want to hold onto it a bit longer.

"Why do you want to give this to me? You know Christianity and I don't get along that well. I'd probably put it in some drawer somewhere and forget I even had it. You should keep it."

"No, I want you to have it and carry it with you until you find someone you feel you should give it to."

"Can you picture me giving a cross to someone?" trying to convince him to keep it. I have nothing against Christianity, but I haven't practiced it at all and never felt it was for me.

"I need you to do this for me as I won't be able to give it to anyone else." At this point he was beginning to cough more, and his color was changing.

"Okay, I'll do what you ask but you need to rest for a while."

"I'll be able to rest quite a bit where I'm going. I want you to wear this cross until you find somebody. Do it for someone who cares a lot about you and wants to give you something to remember him by. It's the best gift that I can give you. We've been through a lot and now you'll be going on by yourself, so this way you'll be carrying me with you." He was getting weaker by the second now and I felt totally helpless.

"You have my word that I'll wear it until I find someone."

"Thanks, you're the best friend that I ever had . . ." and with that, he passed away. With tears in my eyes, I did as he requested and put the cross on my neck.

I checked out the area and realized that we weren't far from our base. In the dark we had no way of knowing where or in what direction we were running. So, I went back to Steve and gently as I could, lifted him over my shoulder. I gathered his stuff along with mine and began hiking for the camp. About four miles later, there it was.

I placed Steve down near the hospital tent making sure the people there would take care of him and reported it to my sergeant. After giving him my report and explaining what happened to Steve, I went to my tent and collapsed.

After what I thought was only a couple of minutes, I awoke to find darkness outside my tent and checking my watch found I'd been asleep for hours. I jumped up to find the camp asleep and only the sentries awake and patrolling the perimeter. There was still a couple of hours before daylight, so I sat down and looked at the cross I now wear.

It wasn't as big as the crosses I've seen clergy people wear but it wasn't tiny either. It seemed made from just one piece of wood and carved very well. It had rounded edges and three or four nicks on them. I had no idea how old it was. Being worn down as it was, it looked pretty good for a cross but then again, how would I know? Thinking of Steve overwhelmed me.

I must have fallen asleep again because the next thing I knew the camp was bustling with everyone getting up, getting breakfast and getting ready to fall in for muster.

"Fall in" the sergeant yelled, and we all nearly fell over each other to get in line.

"We're packing up the camp and moving out, so grab all your gear and report to your division leaders on the double! Dismissed!"

We all fell into marching columns and left the area following our leaders with no idea about where we were going or when we would get there. We stopped for a short lunch and then proceeded on for the rest of the afternoon. At about 5:00 PM we began to hear distant noise coming from large guns and realized that we were approaching the front lines.

Our Sargent called a halt, and we set up camp near a small stream nearby. After chow, we fell in. The Sargent told us we'd be going into combat in the morning and to get plenty of rest as we'd need it. I always had trouble sleeping when I knew we'd be in a battle the next day, so I just sat there thinking about Steve and some of the things we talked about over the last couple of years.

He had always talked about a cross that his family had carried for ages with one generation passing it down to the next. His tone was always reverent when he talked about it. According to Steve, none of his family had ever been pastors or missionaries or religious fanatics but for some reason, they revered this cross. Not being a Christian led me to think that this was just a group of people who treasured this cross for sentimental reasons. Steve, however, took this cross seriously and had a strong, abiding love for his savior, Jesus Christ. He felt that the cross was a real reminder to him of what Jesus had done 2000 years ago. I always listened patiently and tried to nod at the right times.

He was never married and as far as I knew didn't have a girlfriend to write to. None of his family were alive and he was alone. When he talked about his future after the war he apparently had no specific plans. Sitting here now, maybe I should have listened a little closer to some of these conversations. I stuck the cross back inside my t-shirt and after a while, I fell asleep.

Waking up the next morning felt weird because when getting ready for a battle, Steve was always there saying small prayers for us and calming my nerves. He'd hold his cross in his hands and smile. Now there was no Steve, and the distant gun noise was getting louder. Shaking off what used to be, I got my things together and headed out with the "new" feeling of having that cross of Steve's hanging around my neck. Even though it was under my shirt, I felt that everyone could see it. It was the strangest feeling I've ever had.

We all had breakfast and formed up in columns of two and marched out of camp and toward the noise. I was walking next to a guy in the outfit I knew but it wasn't Steve. I smiled weakly at him and continued marching.

After a few miles, we climbed up a steep hill and when we got to the top there was the battle already in process. It was spread across a large valley and there was no way to tell who was gaining the advantage. Sarge told us to hold up here and await orders. We all looked at each other and said nothing as the Sarge disappeared into some trees to our right.

It wasn't long before Sarge came and told us to move out.

We followed him down the hill and toward the front edge of those trees on our right. The noise was deafening with cannon fire, bombs, rifles, and men screaming. They were all going at the same time and yet I could hear each one individually. There was too much happening around me to even think of anything else. Not even the thought of Steve not being there occurred to me. Fear, however, did find a place in my head and seemed to be reigning supreme.

"Get to work digging a bunker. We're the support troops if the battle starts climbing this hill. Under no circumstance are they to overrun us. Now get busy, we don't have a lot of time!" Funny how a sergeant's voice can cut right through just about anything.

About an hour later we had a shallow trench dug; deep enough for us to lay behind. There were about 150 of us and after the Sarge spaced us along the trench we would be able to cover the entire length of the wooded area. We continued digging with the thought that the deeper we went, the safer we would be.

Sure enough, later that afternoon, the battle did indeed draw closer and closer to us. Tim, Fred, and I had managed to dig our hole deep enough to almost stand in and still be able to see over the top. As we looked down the valley, we could see that our side was slowly retreating in our direction and as we looked at each other, we realized that change in our lives was coming and there was nothing we could do about it.

As I leaned forward into our makeshift hole, I could feel Steve's cross on my chest and for some reason I felt a little safer knowing that it was there. It was only a piece of wood but to Steve it was something much more and maybe that's why I felt the way I did. All I know was that I was glad I had it with me.

The minutes dragged on and after an hour our troops were beginning to push the enemy back down the hill, but just barely.

It wasn't a couple of minutes later large explosions happened all around our troops and they began to run in our direction. The explosions were getting closer to us, and our people, what was left of them, were jumping over our makeshift barricade, and hitting the ground behind us. That's when we saw the enemy coming up the valley toward us.

We opened fire but there were so many of them that we were soon overrun. Things went black and all memories of what was going on or what had happened vanished.

I woke up with a nurse looking at me and welcoming me back. My chest felt like something had crashed against it and it was SORE! I asked her what had happened, and she reached over to the small table next to my bed and handed an object to me. It was my cross, but it had a bullet lodged and slightly wrapped around the long leg of the cross, but it didn't break the wood. My chest had a huge black and blue bruise where the cross was while it hung from my neck.

I lay there looking at that cross and thinking of Steve while the nurse told me that the cross saved my life. She told me that only a few of our 150 guys made it through the battle, but reinforcements from our rear guard had got there in time to help us win the battle and drive the enemy back. That was a week ago! I had been out cold all that time. Other than a couple of broken ribs, I would pull through.

She also told me that the war was over . . . that battle had finished their resolve. They had thrown everything they had at us and failed.

Thank goodness, I now get to go home!

Now, forty years later I am telling this story to my son and showing him the cross. I had accepted Christ years ago and have never regretted a moment of it. I wanted him to know that when I leave here someday the cross would be his. I also made sure I gave him the same instructions that Steve had given me along with the history behind it.

I had researched Steve's background and found his genealogy and there was mention in his records of a cross coming into the family some five generations before Steve, but no record of how the cross came to be part of their family line, only that it was passed down to every generation with the same instructions. Steve was the last of their family tree.

Someday, I'll get to thank Steve in person when I join him in heaven.

Chapter Eight
So Now What?

Minstrels sing a song
While artists in silence paint
Searching for the truth

Words lift a soul up
If written with hearts in mind
Longing to show love

A life worth living
Leaves a beautiful trail
We all want to find

Once you weigh anchor,
Home behind, the sea ahead,
Pray for the journey

I don't want you to think I spent all my time lamenting the loss of people in my life. Being born and dying in this world is the life we have. Losing people leaves scars that don't go away. Those scars and memories take up special places in our hearts for us to visit sometimes, not to dwell there, but to remember, smile and move on. Each one was a moment for learning. It's what we choose to do with our lives that matters. Scars are not just defeats; they are victories too.

There are so many things that God created and placed in this world for us to check out that it would take several lifetimes to cover them all. That includes waterfalls, mountains, valleys, oceans, trees, flowers, and don't forget, other people. We can choose to hide from it all or get involved.

Most mornings, I ask the Lord to use me in whatever way He sees fit during the day. Sometimes He really surprises me. I will start a painting usually with a sketch, either on the canvas directly or in a separate sketchbook. This particular time, however, I had drawn out a still life that I wanted to use for a Christmas card that year. The sketch looked good, so I started. By the time I was finished, my still life turned into Bethlehem painted in a modern art style with the nativity instead of the realistic style I had in mind with candles and the Bible. I love the process, and the process is everything, because I know He is in control. The painting was used for our Christmas card that year and sold before the season was over. The lady who bought it, bought it for her son who loved modern art but didn't know the Lord. When he received it, he liked it so much he had it framed and has it hanging in his house for all to see. Who knows how God will use it. You never know what God has in mind with your life. You need to be open enough to let Him work in it.

I am not sure why this is, but nobody wants to ever be forgotten after they pass away. People have tombstones made up or statues or monuments erected in their honor (the bigger, the better). Generals and statesmen have huge artwork erected with all kinds of celebrations to commemorate the occasion just to be remembered. All of us want to leave behind something for people to remember us be it large or small. For me it's people who saw enough of God's work in me to want the same for themselves.

By the Light of a
Single Candlestick

By the light of a single candlestick
The moon shines beside the clouds
Cassiopeia in the night sky
Looking down on the world below
Sees a small, shining ray of hope
From the light of a single candlestick

By the light of a single candlestick
I write the words I want to keep
That carried me over the worst of life
For someone to find when I am gone
So maybe they won't trip in the dark
Using the light of a single candlestick

By the light of a single candlestick
My time here has come to an end
May the roads brighten before you
As you allow God to shine within
Do not worry about where I am
I'm in the light of a single candlestick

By the light of a single candlestick
Go, find your way to the door
You won't trip where the light shines
Nor will you wander off the road
With the love of God, I send you off
By the light of a single candlestick

Tears of Stone

Tears of stone
Shed alone
Landing on
The edge of time

Who can cry
These tears of stone
With hearts that break
As they hit the rocky ground,
Those who choose to cry alone
Allowing no one to show the way

Tears of stone
Can change to gold
When their hearts care
To seek the Divine

The Sin Inside

(inspired by a sermon by Chip McGee)

For us to climb the highest mountains
For us to cross the deepest seas
We need to see the sin inside
And fight that sin upon our knees

To win is not the reason why
To hate only blinds the mind
To kill, leaves you lost, alone
Love's a treasure you must find

Wisdom has the answer, it screams
From the mountains and the seas
We need to see the sin inside
And fight that sin upon our knees

Night Watch

Night is approaching
Sun is going down
Clouds in the distance
Birds make no sound
Solitude and stillness
Fill the Autumn air
Colors of the world
Fade in dark despair
Lightning bugs gather
Floating through the night
Darkness gains in size
Daylight is going by
Standing in the tower
Staring at the fading day
You stand posted alone
Assigned the duty you have
Lives of all beneath you
Depend on what you say
Curling in their blankets
Safe within houses they lay
The light at last is gone
The watch has now begun
Praying for peace and solitude
Until the night is done

Chapter Nine
Hard Won Wisdom
& Experiences

Roses can be dropped
When a thorn gets in the way
There's risk and reward

The cost of freedom
And the price of admission
Will let a soul fly

Don't look to the grave
To be your destination
Look up to the Lord

Find your blessings here
Sharing your road with others
Arrive with blest friends

Aging also makes you appreciate the things around you that you hadn't paid that much attention to in the past. Certain things seem to have more meaning now than they used to. Things you see that are out of place and people doing things that are out of character for them. Symbols seem to mean a little more than they previously did. I love sunrises and sunsets. I love learning more about what God is up to and appreciating His love for me.

I like visiting places where epic things happened or where people I care about have been before me. You can't see their trail, but somehow you feel a presence . . . probably a mind thing (who knows?) It's a special feeling which is hard to explain.

But God

Glasses can be filled
Half empty or half full
And will last a lifetime
If very carefully used

However

It is hard to fill a glass
That lies broken on the floor
Pieces lying here and there
Beyond all hope of yesterday
Promises were many
Before the fall
A world very different today

We are vessels to be filled
Half empty or half full
We'll last the life God gives
If very carefully used

However

It is hard to fill a life
That lies broken on the floor
Pieces lying here and there
Beyond all hope of yesterday
Promises were many
Before the fall
A world very different today

However
But God

A Fallen Rose

A fallen rose someone picked up
From the dust and dirt of the road
Maybe dropped
Or thrown away
There in the mud, a story untold

A rose of matchless beauty
That someone once desired
Left with the weary
And the broken
Fuel eventually for a fire

Maybe rejected
Or thrown aside
Maybe wanted
Or left behind
Maybe needed
Or abandoned
Maybe once loved
Or weeded out

A fallen rose covered with grime
Picked up, washed off, cared for
Saved from the path
Where it was left
Alone,
Who could ask for more?

America

Eagles can soar
Only where they're free to fly
Above the mountains
Above the trees
Above the lakes
Among the clouds in the sky

Freedom is never free
Freedom comes with a cost
America is built on nothing less
Then on backs of patriots lost

The stars and stripes will proudly soar
Only where it's free to fly
Above the mountains
Above the trees
Above the lakes
Among the clouds in the sky

Chapter Ten

Stories & Such

The sounds in the swamp
Come from large and small alike
Carry through the night

So where will you stand
When the sun dies in the sky
Coated by darkness

When forced to leave home
Against all that you believe
Will you stand or cry

Roads can be rocky
Filled with jagged holes unseen
Use the light of God

You learn a lot while you are living out a lifetime. Sometimes you wish you had several lifetimes to live to be able to do all you want to accomplish with the one lifetime you are allowed. The problem is, if we could live several lifetimes to do everything we want to do, we would find more and more things to do which will never end.

There are days when you just sit and do absolutely nothing, you don't feel like doing anything, don't want to do it even if you thought of something to do, and it really doesn't matter how it went even if you did get up to do it. Other days, there are not enough minutes in the day to accomplish all you want to do, but you try anyway and collapse that night in bed exhausted.

Sometimes the time we have is taken away by others. For instance, jury duty (I did 2 years on a Federal Grand Jury), military service (I did 4 years active and 2 inactive in the Navy) or as kids having to go to school for 13 years (if you didn't repeat any grades). Some of us choose to go to college for either 2 years or 4 years, or those who spend even more time for a master's degree (like I did), etc. Those of us who have jobs spend 40 hours or more working every week. If you add the required sleep we need of about 6-8 hours a night, you find that your life seems to be already lived for you. Sounds fair, RIGHT?

That's why what you do with the time you have is so vital, you only get a certain amount and that's it! It's your choice.

Five Dollar Bill

How far have I ridden?
Down valleys, over mountains
Following this rocky path
Looking for land
Not ruined by man
My horse, my gun,
And a five-dollar bill
Is all that's left to call my own

I served in your army
Fought for causes, counted my losses
Victory had a hollow sound
Buried my wife
Buried my son
My horse, my gun,
And a five-dollar bill
Is all that's left to call my own

So, am I strong enough?
To climb mountains, where eagles fly
Where can I finally lie down?
Sorry my friend
No fences to mend
My horse, my gun,
And a five-dollar bill
Is all that's left to call my own

Am I run to ground?
Things I missed; roads not taken
Left me where I am now

Here all alone
Of this I know
My horse, my gun,
And a five-dollar bill
Is all that's left to call my own

Have I missed the mark?
I'll probably never know
The Spirit of Heaven's a hound
Who fastens my soul
And calls me home
My horse, my gun,
And a five-dollar bill
Is all that's left to call my own

When You find my grave in years to come
Along a trail unknown
I, my horse, and my gun,
Will all be gone
Check my clothes,
It may still be there
Creased and torn, unspent and worn
You're sure to find my five-dollar bill

The Heather and The Stone

You will find it there between
The heather and the stone
The browns and the greens
Sadness and memories
People and places lost to me

I left the land the first of May
The heather and stones
The ponds and lakes
Places where I played
Left them behind
To sail around the world
For riches I knew I'd find

More holes in my clothes than cash
I worked many a field
And sailed many a sea
Joining many in the dance
Til there was little left of me
In my hunting for riches
Where grass promised to be green

One by one they all left
Friends who paid a price
Having searched in vain
Gone like a forgotten song
Leaving behind what they knew
For they all thought for sure
There was gold in oceans of blue

My years now behind me
I've little to my name
My dreams of all that wealth
I tossed into the sea
I'm going to the land of my youth
To settle these bones down
My roving days are through

Looking out over my land
My house, my friends, gone
A cruel war had come
And burned all that I had known
Since I had left this all behind
I now have to start over again
My treasure lies in the ground

You will find it between
The heather and the stone
The browns and the greens
Sadness and memories
Where new hope waits for me

The Bayou

The bayou always has something to say
You are not the first to float through its trees
You will not find anything marking the way
Just the noise from the birds and the bees
A splash in the water will not bother your day
Its' the ones you don't hear that cause alarm
Do not let the beauty lead you astray
For when you do, you may come to harm

The world within the water is alive
Never think that you are there alone
Every log you see laying on its side
May not be a mossy log at all
As you're floating listen for the sounds
Of birds and animals up in the trees
If the sounds ever stop, and all is still
Look ahead, look behind, above and beneath

Many a canoe has floated in the swamp
And many have come back alone
Bearing scars that were not there before
Telling only what the bayou knows
Think it through and think it well
Before you decide to take your leave
The bayou always has something to say
You are not the first to float through its trees

I Don't Miss the Whales

I loved the wind
Dancing in the sky
Moving all the sails
Skimming on the water
Now I live my life
On the hills by the sea
And I don't miss the whales

Day after day
Months at a time
I stood beneath the sails
Living on the edge of
A world of foam and grace
With the wind and the gales

Our ship was old
Many a mile she
Pushed along by the sails
People live and die
The same is true of ships
And I don't miss the whales

We heard a sound
"He's off the port bow!"
Hailed from among the sails
We could not wait
To see him for ourselves
We hung onto the rails

We shot the gun
"It's a direct hit!"
Came the voice from the sails
Our ship was turning
Though not of its own will
And I don't miss the whales

A reef was there
Just under the waves
A curse to ships with sails
A noise, quite loud
Swept us off our feet
Falling with ropes and pails

The line then snapped
Our prize escaped
Masts crashed with the sails
With no chance for help
Our ship sank into the sea
And I don't miss the whales

I am now alone
The crew is gone
No more to live with sails
I watch the ships
Set sail on the deep blue sea
And pray they never fail

It seems so grand
Oceans always call
To live below the sails
So, go with my blessing
I wish you the best of seas
But I won't miss the whales

Pale is the sky
Blue is the ocean
As ships swim with white sails
Bright green blows the grass
All around my bare feet
And I don't miss the whales

Golden Eagle

When first I saw an eagle fly
Standing on a rock by the river
I never knew just being there
What freedom really costs

What is it that drives men
Wanting what they should never have
Time climbing endless ladders
Focused on that very next rung

Wars are founded on greed
Hatred passed from father to son
Not everyone fights for a cause
Many times wrong people die

People dying on every side
Who never got to build a life
Those my heart once held dear
While asking the question, why?

Bullets never get to choose their marks
They only fly until they are stopped

Fathers against sons,
Friend against friend
Drug into wars
We did not ask for
Leaving me to stand alone
To watch the eagle fly

No one had to cry
No one had to die
People like me left behind
Knowing they'll never return

Bullets never get to choose their marks
They only fly until they are stopped

I never thought that I would find
The peace I feel inside
Watching the river flow
Watching an eagle fly

You Own . . .

You own too many trees
Yet always sit in the sun
Looking for other things to gain
Cries for help grow louder
You cover both your ears
Living your precious life in vain

You own too many vineyards
Yet you hate the taste of wine
Looking for other things to gain
The poor sit on roadsides
As you hurry down the street
Living your precious life in vain

You own too many buildings
Yet you have never lived in one
Looking for other things to gain
Churches will fall to ruin
As you hoard all your cash
Living your precious life in vain

Chapter 10A

Christmas

As I've mentioned in previous books, I love Christmas and am always thinking about the different parts of the Christmas story. I just could not let this book go by without something for Christmas. I have shared a poem for Mary earlier, so here is another poem . . . this time about the stable. I am sure that the stables had more than one stall and were used by the various customers of the inn. Our current Christmas cards tend to "clean" up the scene and have Mary and Joseph dressed in fine clothes surrounded by the cleanest hay and well-groomed animals. These old stables were NOT the cleanest places on the Earth, but if you must use one, you use one.

So, this poem is about a chance encounter where someone staying at the inn happened on a once in a lifetime occurrence in an unlikely place.

I Came Across a Manger

I came across a manger
With a baby lying there
A dirty place for one so young
Smell of animals in the air

The baby is a king I hear
Though nary a throne in sight
A dirty place for one so young
Beneath the stars so bright

They had to birth their baby here
Couldn't even afford a room
A dirty place for one so young
Lying here beneath the moon

A family in a stable
Not even vagrants call home
A dirty place for one so young
Facing a future so unknown

I know I must be on my way
But it's hard for me to leave
A dirty place for one so young
It's something I can't believe

I only came to get my mule
Not to walk in on this scene
A dirty place for one so young
Babies in stables . . . obscene

As I leave, I turn around
To see some shepherds walking in
A dirty place for one so young
And they in their rags and skins

They're talking about an angel
And then a multitude of them
A dirty place for one so young
Reaching for the stars over him

Now they're all bowing
Circled around the trough
A dirty place for one so young
Why is it I who feels so lost

Shepherds worshipping a baby
In a stable of all places
A dirty place for one so young
With love flowing from their faces

I wonder if I'll ever know
If this child becomes a king
A dirty place for one so young
Who knows what his future will bring

Late Last Night

Late last night
As the moon went to bed
I prayed for the safety
Only God can give
Dark clouds above
Thunder in the distance
Surrounded by my covers
Sleep offers no resistance

Board By Board

Board by board, water's rising
Board by board, water's rising
Knocked on the door, the door was shut
I pounded on the door, the door was shut
Board by board, water's rising

Opened my eyes to a newborn day
Saw the clouds took the sun away
Looked out my window, my town was gone
Stared out my window, my town was gone
Board by board, water's rising

My house is floating, what can I do
Rain keeps pouring, what he said was true
He said it was coming, but what did I care
He knew it was coming, but what did I care
Board by board, water's rising

Water as far as the eye can see
Why oh why is this happening to me
Nothing on the water but Noah's ole boat
Grabbing onto something hoping I will float
Board by board, water's rising
Board by board, water's rising

Chapter Eleven
Contemplations

Age is a Number
Assigned to map out our lives
And then forgotten

To worry or not
What our tomorrows may bring
Can make days unsure

Make your choices well
You get to do this just once
Seek the right answers

Since you have a life
Decide how you will live it
Will you sink or swim?

This is where I get to contemplate my future within all these thoughts. We never know if there is one minute, one hour, one day, one week or one year or more left to our existence. Unless a monument is erected for us, or a painting, a poem, a book, or a song for people in the future to see and contemplate. Within a generation, we'll be forgotten. No one likes that idea, but there it is.

These are all physical reminders of us and our lives, but each one will eventually pass away leaving nothing of our existence. Those of us who are artists, songwriters, builders or writers hope that, at least, some of our work will be appreciated generations from now but it's a very long shot. So, why do we spend our time creating things if we know they're not going to last?

Some people do it for fame, wanting as many people as possible to know them or know about them. Some do it to sell to others who do not or cannot do it themselves. Some do it to brighten up their surroundings or the surroundings of others. Some want to make statements that may improve the common good, both now and in the future.

As I mentioned earlier, seeing my work hung on a wall, any wall, was and is a big deal for me and hopefully other for people who may enjoy it also. It's not totally a vanity thing, (Look at MY work up there, aren't I great?) though there is some of that (in various amounts depending on the person). Whichever way it goes, at least I had a chance to express something that was inside and got it outside of me for others to see and judge. Just be careful of the work you exhibit. Every time we have a work of art set up for display, we take a chance that those who see it may ridicule it and in turn, ridicule us.

There was a young man in the fifth grade in one of my Sunday School classes who had taken a brand-new study book I had given to each of the students which had a picture of Jesus on the cover and drew in nails, lightning bolts, etc. all over the face of Jesus. When he showed up with it for the next class, I noticed it, but didn't say anything. Instead, I shared with the class that I was an artist who knew that everything I create and put on a wall is judged by whoever goes by. I can't be there to explain what I meant when I created it and each of these people who sees my work in the future will judge me based on what they see on the wall, nothing else. I have no control over that. The following week, this fifth grader came back into class with every one of his alterations on the face of Jesus erased and cleaned up the best he could. I never said a word about it . . . didn't have to.

God gave me the talents to create things, to beautify things and to try to make my world a better place to live while I'm here. I have long since given up any notion of creating a name for myself. Now I'm focused on what I can do for others and what God can do through me.

These books of poetry I've written will one day disappear as will I. That doesn't bother me at all because I'm confident that I know where I'm going and I'm hoping that all these talents that God has graciously given me and used for His purposes will affect others to know that Jesus is, indeed, the only way to Heaven for this generation and for all the generations to come. My hope is that for as long as my work lasts, God will be able to use it.

The Minstrel

Follow the sound of the wind to
Where the Minstrel used to play
Among the trees he sang to
The flowers everyday
The stream danced nearby to
Add notes of its own
They all joined together to
Sing the old Creation Song

Follow the sound of the wind to
Where the Minstrel used to stand
Where melodies filled the breeze to
Where the harmonies lent a hand
And all the music led to
The saving of our souls
There among the trees to
Sing the old Creation Song

Follow the sound of the wind to
Where the Minstrel used to stand
I can no longer be there to
Sing my heart to Him
God has me in another place to
Shout and dance along
To sing His praises every day to
Sing the old Creation Song

Sing the song while you can
Singing words to show the way
For soon your days will cycle down
And then you will need
A Minstrel in your place

Sing the old Creation song
Guide the hearts along the way
Follow the sound of the wind to
Where trees stand and sway to
Be the Minstrel in my place

For You

If I could write a song
That would bring me
Close to You
I could never stop
I would never stop
Writing songs for You

If I could live my life
That would draw others
Close to You
I could never stop
I would never stop
Living my life for You

Memories

Memories are
Living
Breathing thoughts
Calling you
Back to mind

Jeremiah 6:16

When the dark wood rose
Just beyond the hill
The moon had slipped
Just behind a cloud
All was dark and still

Mile after mile
A long journey made
Wanting to reach my goal
My eyes feeling heavy
Distant mountains fade

The path leads into the woods
What did Jeremiah say
Stand still and consider
Am I on the beaten path
Or am I led astray

No one here to ask
So, I will camp where I am
When I've had some sleep
And fully awake to see
I'll assess what I can

I will kneel and pray
To see what God has to say
There is peace on His road
Direction for my soul
Guidance throughout my day

The wood is not so dark
During the light of the day
Knowing where I'm going
Owned and blessed by God
Speeds me on my way

Times Like These

Along the shore I see birds flying by
Silhouettes against a fading sky
Here I see a world at peace
God-given beauty for me to see

Gentle waves rolling along the shore
Pulling the sand, then bringing back more
Dancing with the late-day breeze
God-given beauty for me to see

Times like these
Hide between
A thought and a dream
Seek them out
If only once
If only today
For times like these
Only hide between
A thought and a dream

Palm trees swaying to and fro
Standing in the sand on the shore
Sounds of waves breaking at sea
God-given beauty for me to see

Chapter Twelve
Parting Thoughts

Living and writing
Painting and singing our songs
Lifts us from the ground

Who holds the future
Except the same God I love
The firm hope of all

Bring light to darkness
Let everyone see his love
In all that you do

Believe and belong
What Jesus says still holds true
Trust his love for you

I almost never get to choose what I'll write or how I'll write. I would love to be able to sit down and write as many writers do. They will put in an hour or two at a set time every day. That is not me (I've tried it . . . nothing). I can be doing almost anything at any time of the day when a word or words pop into my head and I write them down. By themselves they don't say a lot, but later, when other words show up, they get paired up and begin to make sense. Some ideas sit around for years before something comes along where I can then use them. I've learned to love the surprises and to marvel at writing them down. Many of the words speak to me along the way as I hope by my sharing them with you blesses you.

Many of the ideas this time around came from other people in ministry through sermons, prayers, or things that they did. It was as much of a surprise to them as the ideas were to me. And they thought I wasn't listening :>)

I ended my last book wondering if I would ever get to write another one. I don't have to wonder any more. Thank you, Lord, for this opportunity and I pray that you use this as you will.

This last group of poems are a mixed bag, some funny, some serious . . . enjoy! As with my other books, I have prayed for those of you who took the time to read this book and hoped that you were able to get something out of it that will change your lives, a little or a lot.

Blessings, Al

Dancing on my Bed

Dancing on my bed
Free as a bird
Light as a feather
Jumping ever higher
But never too high
Excitement within
Waving arms without
Loving every minute
Until my mom comes in

If

If those who are part
Of Satan's army
Knew the future that lies
In wait for them
And knew who they were
Fighting against
I believe
His army would be no more

A River Runs Through Me

A river runs through me
For once at the dam
I plugged the holes
Now the dam is gone
That's the way it goes

I'm Told

I'm told
I always need to
Turn the other cheek

And so, I did that

Now I'm thinking about it
As I lie here
Facing up at the sun

Bible Math

One mansion waiting on a hill
Two little feet to carry me there
Three Wise Men following a star
Four bold Gospels we need to share
Five books that Moses wrote
Six days of work, then sabbath we're told
Seven candles shining on a stand
Eight lonely people riding an ark
Nine lowly lepers who never gave thanks
Ten new commandments we need to learn
Eleven bright stars to Joseph was shown
Twelve disciples that Jesus had chose

One Bible written to get me home

The Dance

One by one, He danced them all away
The pain, the guilt, the lies, the hate
When God dances
Over my soul
Even so
The pain, the guilt, the lies, the hate
One by one, He dances them all away

A Fire in My Heart

Like a fire in my heart
Where time never wants to end
Where the shadows on the wall
Dance forever
As long as the fire glows

Where ideas can be born
If they cross the great divide
Exposing to the world
Something that's new
Changing it forever

Printed in the United States
by Baker & Taylor Publisher Services